Dedicated to the memory
of my dear friend,
Sister Gertrude Vaccaro,
who gave comfort and inspiration
to all who knew her
and gave of herself freely
to the Service of the Lord.

"Thou hast made us, O Lord,
for Thyself and our heart
shall find no rest
till it rest in Thee."

St. Augustine

Salesian Missions wishes to thank those who have given their kind permission to reprint
material included in this book. Every effort has been made to give proper acknowledgements. Any omissions or errors are deeply regretted, and the publisher, upon notification,
will be pleased to make necessary corrections in subsequent editions.

ACKNOWLEDGEMENTS: "Worthwhile" and "You Never Can Tell," by Ella Wheeler
Wilcox, "Prayer for a Day's Walk" by Grace N. Crowell, "The Dreaded Task" by Margaret
E. Bruner, reprinted from POEMS THAT TOUCH THE HEART by A.L. Alexander by
permission of Louise Alexander. "God is in Every Tomorrow" by Laura A. Barter Snow
from THE BEST LOVED RELIGIOUS POEMS by James Gilchrist Lawson reprinted by
permission. "Adoration, Praise and Thanksgiving" by Elizabeth Craven, "Thankfulness"
by Adelaide Anne Proctor, "Resolve" by Ella Wheeler Wilcox from LINES TO LIVE BY
© 1972 by Clinton T. Howell, published by Thomas Nelson, Inc. reprinted by permission
of Clinton T. Howell. "Prayers Can't be Answered Unless They Are Prayed" by Helen
Steiner Rice reprinted by permission of Gibson Greeting Cards, Inc., Cincinnati, Ohio
45327. "Life is Worth Living" reprinted from POEMS TO INSPIRE by Nick Kenny by permission of T.S. Denison & Co., Inc. "Your Own Version" by Paul Gilbert reprinted from
THE TREASURE CHEST by permission of Dr. Charles L. Wallis.

Best Loved Poems

from the Salesian Collection

Compiled and Edited by
Sara Tarascio

Illustrated by
Marion L. Quimby

CONTENTS

Never be discouraged 6

An Evening Hope 7

Open My Eyes 8

God's Plans 9

Sunshine 10

You Never Can Tell 11

Second Sight 12

Rest 14

Just to be Alive
   Is Worth a "Thank You" . . 15

From "Roofs" 16

When Winter Comes 17

Climbing 18

Polite Prayer 19

Kindness 20

Minutes of Gold 21

Be Near Me, Lord 22

Resolve 23

Can You Say? 24

I Lift the Branch 25

The Highest Good 26

Prayer 27

God is in every tomorrow . . . 28

Day by Day 29

Adoration, Praise and
   Thanksgiving 30

God's Voice 32

Dreams and Deeds 33

I Know You're There 34

Day by Day 36

Home 39

The House of Prayer 40

Worth While 41

God Bless You 43

Prayers Can't be Answered
   Unless They Are Prayed . . 44

Today 46

Tell Him So 47

The Passing Years 48

Mountain Te Deum 50

Just For Today 51

Life's Adventure 52

God Understands 54

Deeper 55

Assurance 56

Dream Dreams 57

If Just One Soul 58

God's Love 59

A Morning Prayer 60

Only Trust Him 61

This Day 62

The Meaning 63

Steadfast Heart 64

Be True 66

The Hardest Thing 68

Life is Worth Living 70

Help Me 71

The Dreaded Task 72

It Matters Not 73

Loneliness 74

Prayer for a Day's Walk 76

The Artist 78

The Little Road 79

Lead Thou the Way 80

Lifeline 81

Teach us, Lord 82

The Weaver 83

Thankfulness 84

The Loving Thing 87

Rest Thou My Mind 88

Confession 90

Autograph 92

Human Frailty 93

Open My Eyes 94

There is One Who Knows 97

Yesterday's Cross 98

Needless Worry 99

A Morning Offering 100

Blessing on All Our Days 101

We Thank Thee 102

Life 103

God's Design 104

Morning Prayer 105

God Promised 106

Use Me Lord 107

Keep Me Near Thee 108

Life's Seasons 109

Understanding 110

Extra Things 111

Make Life a Little Sweeter 112

Sharing 113

Thou Art Near 114

Experience 115

Kindness 116

Never Alone 117

These Are the Gifts I Ask 119

Consolation 120

Thank God for Little
   Things 121

Choice 122

The Human Touch 123

Hymn 124

A Guide that Never Falters . . 125

My Task 126

You Never Walk Alone 127

Your Own Version 128

Never be discouraged
When failures come to light —
Just use them for stepping stones
And make a stronger fight.

Loreta Inman

An Evening Hope

I sat in the quiet evening hour
    As the lengthening shadows grew,
And my gaze was fixed on parting sun
    In a change of the gentlest hue.

And I could not help but contemplate
    On the close of another day,
That the end of the day has a beauty, too,
    As the morning light's first ray.

And so it is in the life we live,
    Though moments be weary or long,
At end of the day, the sun's parting ray
    Brings the gentle evening song.

I have lived my day on earth below,
    And now with the evening's rays,
I can know no fear but expectant hope,
    For my trust is in Christ, the Way.

And though lengthening shadows round me twine,
    I will never fear the night;
To the golden hues of my Heavenly home,
    I am guided by Christ, my Light.

                    Charles G. Ramsey

Open My Eyes

God open my eyes so I may see
    And feel Your presence close to me...
Give me strength for my stumbling feet
    As I battle the crowd
        on life's busy street,
And widen the vision of my unseeing eyes
    So in passing faces I'll recognize
Not just a stranger, unloved and unknown,
    But a friend with a heart
        that is much like my own...
Give me perception to make me aware
    That scattered profusely
        on life's thoroughfare
Are the best gifts of God
        that we daily pass by
    As we look at the world
        with an unseeing eye.

Helen Steiner Rice

God's Plans

God's plans are like the ocean,
    Varied as the winds that fall—
All the products of His wisdom,
    All are subject to His call.
Not a breeze that stirs the tempest—
    Or a sparrow down doth fall,
But our Heavenly Father knoweth—
    For He watches over all.

Elizabeth E.S. Williams

Sunshine

Come out into the sunlight,
    Heart of mine;
Why linger in the shadows
    And repine!

Winter's snows can't last forever,
    Neither pain;
Oh, come out into the sunlight
    Once again!

In the blue the birds are singing
    Up above;
Throw away thy gloom and sadness
    All is love!

Oh, come out into the sunshine,
    Soul of mine;
Never wert thou made for darkness,
    Life is thine!

Ralph Spaulding Cushman
From THE MESSAGE OF STEWARDSHIP

You Never Can Tell

You never can tell when you send a word
    Like an arrow shot from a bow
By an archer blind, be it cruel or kind,
    Just where it may chance to go.
It may pierce the breast of your dearest friend,
    Tipped with its poison or balm,
To a stranger's heart in life's great mart
    It may carry its pain or its calm.

You never can tell when you do an act
    Just what the result will be,
But with every deed you are sowing a seed,
    Though the harvest you may not see.

Each kindly act is an acorn dropped
    In God's productive soil;
You may not know, but the tree shall grow
    With shelter for those who toil.

You never can tell what your thoughts will do
    In bringing you hate or love,
For thoughts are things, and their airy wings
    Are swifter than carrier doves.
They follow the law of the universe —
    Each thing must create its kind,
And they speed o'er the track to bring you back
    Whatever went out from your mind.

Ella Wheeler Wilcox

Second Sight

I cannot weave a tapestry,
Whose vibrant colors gleam,
But I can thread a needle,
And sew a little seam.
I have no silver notes to turn
Into a lovely song,
But I can sit and listen
To the tune and hum along.

I cannot preach a sermon,
To edify the year,
But I can say a little prayer,
The Lord can always hear.

I cannot climb a mountain,
All wreathed in clouds of white,
But I can walk a woodland path,
And feel my heart grow light.

I cannot paint a masterpiece,
I cannot carve in stone,
But there is something I can do,
That is my very own.
For though I do not weave or climb,
Nor paint, or carve, or sing,
Somehow I find a bit of God,
...In every living thing.

Grace E. Easley

Rest

Are you very weary? Rest a little bit.
In some quiet corner, fold your hands
and sit.
Do not let the trials that have grieved
you all the day
Haunt this quiet corner; drive them
all away!
Let your heart grow empty of every
thought unkind
That peace may hover round you, and
joy may fill your mind.
Count up all your blessings, I'm sure
they are not few,
That the dear Lord daily just bestows
on you.
Soon you'll feel so rested, glad you
stopped a bit,
In this quiet corner, to fold your
hands and sit.

Just to be Alive
is Worth a
"Thank You"...

Accept, dear Lord,
from this unasking heart
a staunchless well of gratitude;
All that creation can afford
is mine — at least in part.
Joy or pain—
from Thy hands —
all is good.

G.M. Carr

from "Roofs"

They say that life is a highway
    and its milestones are the years,
And now and then there is a tollgate
    where you buy your way with tears.
It's a rough road and a steep road
    and it stretches broad and far,
But at least it leads to a golden town
    where golden houses are.

                Joyce Kilmer

When Winter Comes

When winter comes into our lives
    With its uncertain sound,
To strip us of our warmth and joy,
    Our petals on the ground,
We may be tempted to give up;
    To fold beneath life's storm.
We may be tempted to forsake
    The hope which keeps us warm.
But, we must learn to stand up tall;
    To always face the sun
And patiently await the day
    When winter's work is done.
For winter winds will cease to howl,
    The snows will melt away,
Then we shall see the beauty of
    Another summer's day.
And we will have renewed our strength
    When summer's wind first blows,
For God will whisper once again
    The promise of a rose.

Glenda Fulton Davis

Climbing

Feeling the wind on my face,
Climbing the mountain height,
Walking beneath the stars alone,
Seeing beauty in the night —
Rising above the earth to dream,
Hearing moonlight's melody,
I must believe with all my heart
God will work out the dawn for me!

Marion Schoeberlein

Polite Prayer

The polite part
of speaking
with God
is to be still
long enough
to listen.

Edward Gloeggler

Kindness

A little word in kindness spoken,
    A motion, or a tear,
Has often healed the heart that's broken
    And made a friend sincere.

A word, a look, has crushed to earth
    Full many a budding flower,
Which, had a smile but owned its birth,
    Would bless life's darkest hour.

Then deem it not an idle thing
    A pleasant word to speak;
The face you wear, the thought you bring,
    A heart may heal or break.

John Greenleaf Whittier

Minutes of Gold

Two or three minutes — two or three hours,
What do they mean in this life of ours?
Not very much if but counted as time,
But minutes of gold and hours sublime,
If only we'll use them once in a while
To make someone happy — make someone smile.

A minute may dry a little lad's tears,
An hour sweep aside trouble of years.
Minutes of my time may bring to an end
Hopelessness somewhere, and bring me a friend.

Be Near Me, Lord

Be near me, Lord, each night and day
  And lead me with Your light,
O, keep me in Your loving care,
  And guide my life aright.

Forgive my every sin and fault
  For all the years gone past,
The years ahead I give to You
  However long they last.

I praise You for Your goodness, Lord,
  My heart I give to Thee,
O help me, Lord, to live for You
  Through all the years to be.

Rev. Thomas Foy

Resolve

Build on resolve, and not upon regret,
    the structure of thy future.
Do not grope among the shadows of old sins,
    but let thine own soul's light
    shine on the path of hope
    and dissipate the darkness.

Waste no tears upon the blotted record of lost years,
    but turn the leaf and smile, oh, smile,
    to see the fair white pages that remain for thee.

Prate not of thy repentance, but believe the
    spark divine dwells in thee: let it grow.

That which the upreaching spirit can achieve
    the grand and all-creative forces know;
    they will assist and strengthen as the light
    lifts up the acorn to the oak tree's height.

Thou hast but to resolve, and lo! God's whole
    great universe shall fortify thy soul.

                       Ella Wheeler Wilcox

Can You Say?

Can you say in parting with the day
  that's slipping fast,

That you helped a single person of the
  many you have passed?

Is a single life rejoicing over what you
  did or said?

Does some one whose hopes were fading,
  now with courage look ahead?

Did you waste the day or lose it, was
  it well or poorly spent?

Did you leave a trend of kindness, or a
  scar of discontent?

As you close your eyes in slumber, do you
  think that God would say—

You have made the world much better
  for the life you've lived today?

Cecilia Felsenthal

I Lift The Branch

As I grow older day by day
And heartaches add to wisdom's bay,
The loves for which my youth once vied
No longer light my fires, inside.
I lift the branch that's hanging low.
I smell the rose but let it grow.

Adventure lacks the lure it knew
When foolish dreams and passions grew
And though it still demands my smile
(Where past and present meet awhile)
No more I haunt the turtle's rest
Or flush the robin from her nest.

I journey, now, to meet an end
Where deeds of past the future blend
And what I pass, in love's embrace,
I leave for better in its place—
But God must often hear me say:
I wish I lived my life this way.

Michael Dubina

The Highest Good

To attain the highest good
Of true man and womanhood,
Simply do
your honest best —
God with joy
will do the rest.

James Whitcomb Riley

Prayer

Dear Lord and Father of mankind,
　　Forgive our foolish ways!
Reclothe us in our rightful mind,
In purer lives Thy service find,
　　In deeper reverence, praise.

Drop Thy still dews of quietness,
　　Till all our strivings cease;
Take from our souls the strain and
　　stress,
And let our ordered lives confess
　　The beauty of Thy peace.

John Greenleaf Whittier

God is in every tomorrow,
    Therefore I live for today,
Certain of finding at sunrise,
    Guidance and strength for the way;
Power for each moment of weakness,
    Hope for each moment of pain,
Comfort for every sorrow,
    Sunshine and joy after rain.

Laura A. Barter Snow

Day by Day

Day by day my Shepherd walks beside me;
    Day by day I know His tender care.
And I know whatever shall betide me,
    Christ my Lord goes with me ev'rywhere.

Midst life's storms and through deepest valley,
    His abiding Presence goes before.
I'm assured whatever shall befall me,
    His rich grace my courage shall restore.

Day by day my Saviour's love surrounds me,
    Day by day communion sweet is mine.
And darkest night shall not confound me,
    When I walk with Christ my Lord divine.

Kathryn T. Bowsher

Adoration, Praise, and Thanksgiving

I thank Thee, God, that I have lived
In this great world and known its many joys;
The song of birds, the strong, sweet scent of hay
And the cooling breezes in the secret dusk,
The flaming sunsets at the close of day,
Hills, and the lonely, heather-covered moors,
Music at night, and moonlight on the sea,
The beat of waves upon the rocky shore
And wild, white spray, flung high in ecstasy:
The faithful eyes of dogs, and treasured books,
The love of kin and fellowship of friends,
And all that makes life dear and beautiful.

I thank Thee, too, that there has come to me
A little heartache and the loneliness
That comes with parting, and the word, "Goodbye,"
Dawn breaking after dreary hours of pain,
When I discovered that night's gloom must yield
And morning light break through to me again.
Because of these and other blessings poured
Unasked upon my wondering head,
Because I know that there is yet to come
An even richer and more glorious life,
And most of all, because Thine only Son
Once sacrificed life's loveliness for me—
I thank Thee, God, that I have lived.

Elizabeth Craven

God's Voice

I hear God's voice in the gentle rain
That softly falls on my window pane.
I hear God's voice in the wind that blows
O'er fragrant meadows and winter snows.

I hear God's voice in the heaving sea,
In song of wind and in hum of bee.
I hear God's voice in the hush of night;
At evening's close and in noon's bright light.

I hear God's voice in all mankind,
In childhood's laughter, in gifted mind.
I hear God's voice in the frail and old,
In the strong and vibrant—we make one fold.

The voice speaks ever of peace and love,
Of joy unending in Heaven above.
God made this earth for our delight;
Let us sing His praise by day and night.

Rev. Thomas Foy

Dreams and Deeds

Dear Master, in whose life I see
All that I long and fail to be;
Let thy clear light for ever shine,
To shame and guide this life of mine.

Though what I dream and what I do
In my poor days are always two,
Help me, oppressed by things undone,
O thou, whose dreams and deeds were one.

John Hunter

I Know You're There

I know You're there
    when dawn begins to paint
The skies with color high above my head.
I know You're there when birds begin to sing
In spite of rain, a happy song instead.
I know You're there along the narrow path
That winds beyond the summit of a hill.
And when the twilight falls,
    'neath stars above,
Within the silence I have found You still.

I know You're there
    throughout the busy hours
I scarce have time to whisper Your sweet Name,
When snowflakes turn the winter world to white,
And autumn burns the hills with her bright flame.

I know You're there
   when spring peeps through the ground,
And bluebells softly ripple in the wind,
When summer comes and dappled shadows lend
A quiet peace beyond the river's bend.

I know You're there
   beyond the slightest doubt,
So many times I've felt Your presence when
Doubt blocked the way or when a bridge was out,
And once again You helped me on again.
And through the years when it may well appear
I walk alone and there are none to care,
Dear Lord,
   what breathless joy to turn around,
...And find You there!

         Grace E. Easley

Day by Day

If you have a sack of troubles
That you cannot set aright,
Close beside you through the day,
And long into the night,
If you are sore with sorrow,
From which you cannot flee,
Groping through the shadows,
For a path you cannot see,

If you are disillusioned,
With a lot of faded dreams,
Clutching tarnished treasures
That are splitting at the seams,
Wading through the marshes
Of a bunch of wasted years,
Grasping straws you cannot reach,
and drowning in your tears,

You've got to learn to give before
You earn the right to take,
Who doesn't bend before the wind,
Is mighty apt to break.
Just as a rose needs sunlight,
To nourish tender shoots,
So each of us needs love to grow,
Beginning at the roots.

And if today is cloudy,
Tomorrow might be fine.
No one has ever failed who kept
A happy state of mind.
The longest journey taken,
Starts with a single mile,
And one-day-at-a-time can change
The worthless to worthwhile!

Grace E. Easley

Home

Home is where the heart is,
    you have often heard it said.
Home is where the songbirds sing
    their sweetest, overhead.

Home is like the rainbow's end
    that beckons in the blue.
Home is where your brightest dreams
    take root and all come true.

And yet it's more than just a place
    where people sleep and eat.
A home that's real has something
    indefinable and sweet.

It may be just a cottage
    or a castle with a dome,
But if God dwells within its walls
    it really is a Home!

                Nick Kenny

The House of Prayer

"The House of Prayer"
    is no farther away
Than the quiet spot
    where you kneel and pray.
For the heart is a temple
    when God is there
As you place yourself
    in His Loving Care.

Helen Steiner Rice

40

Worth While

It is easy enough to be pleasant,
    When life flows by like a song,
But the man worth while is one who will smile,
    When everything goes dead wrong.
For the test of the heart is trouble,
    And it always comes with the years,
And the smile that is worth the praises of earth
    Is the smile that shines through tears.

It is easy enough to be prudent,
    When nothing tempts you to stray,
When without or within no voice of sin
    Is luring your soul away;
But it's only a negative virtue
    Until it is tried by fire,
And the life that is worth the honor on earth
    Is the one that resists desire.

By the cynic, the sad, the fallen,
    Who had no strength for the strife,
The world's highway is cumbered today;
    They make up the sum of life.
But the virtue that conquers passion,
    And the sorrow that hides in a smile,
It is these that are worth the homage on earth
    For we find them but once in a while.

Ella Wheeler Wilcox

God Bless You

I seek in prayerful words, dear friend,
    My heart's true wish to send you,
That you may know that, far or near,
    My loving thoughts attend you.

I cannot find a truer word,
    Nor better to address you;
Nor song, nor poem have I heard
    Is sweeter than God bless you!

God bless you! So I've wished you all
    Of brightness life possesses;
For can there any joy at all
    Be yours unless God blesses?

And so, "through all thy days
    May shadows touch thee never—"
But this alone: God bless thee
    Then art thou safe forever.

Prayers Can't Be Answered
Unless They Are Prayed

Life without purpose
    is barren indeed —
There can't be a harvest
    unless you plant seed,
There can't be attainment
    unless there's a goal,
And man's but a robot
    unless there's a soul...
If we send no ships out,
    no ships will come in,
And unless there's a contest,
    nobody can win...
For games can't be won
    unless they are played,
And prayers can't be answered
    unless they are prayed...

So whatever is wrong
    with your life today,
You'll find a solution
    if you kneel down and pray
Not just for pleasure,
    enjoyment and health,
Not just for honors
    and prestige and wealth...
But pray for a purpose
    to make life worth living.
And pray for the joy
    of unselfish giving,
For great is your gladness
    and rich your reward
When you make your life's purpose
    the choice of the Lord.

Helen Steiner Rice

Today

My life is a gift of God given, not in years, but a day at a time. Today is the day the Lord has made for me, and He planned it to be the most important day of my life.

Yesterday is gone, never to return. I must not worry about it, but leave it in the hands of God. Tomorrow and all that it holds is God's secret and its coming is not assured.

Only today is mine. Each day, arranged by God with infinite wisdom and goodness is His gift, His act of love for me. In thanksgiving I will offer Him every day the gift of myself — my prayers, works, joys and sufferings.

Dear Lord, receive it graciously.

Tell Him So

If you hear a kind word spoken
  Of some worthy soul you know,
It may fill his heart with sunshine
  If you only tell him so.

If a deed, however humble,
  Helps you on your way to go,
Seek the one whose hand has helped you,
  Seek him out and tell him so!

If your heart is touched and tender
  Toward a sinner, lost and low,
It might help him to do better
  If you'd only tell him so!

Oh my sisters, oh, my brothers,
  As over life's rough path you go,
If God's love has saved and kept you.
  Do not fail to tell men so!

The Passing Years

Life passes by so fast, Lord,
I know I'm sure to miss
A vital part unless you keep
Reminding me of this.
There's so much that I want to do,
A lot I've left undone,
So many plans discarded,
And a few I've not begun.

Life passes by so fast, Lord,
How often I've been told,
It always does around the time
That we are growing old.
"For everything a season"
Is wise as well as just,
But I had rather wear me out,
Than fall apart with rust.

Life passes by so fast, Lord,
The days, the months, the years,
Lord keep a smile upon my lips,
And blot away the tears.
Teach me to lean upon Your arm,
When pain and sickness strike,
To tell the facts from fancies,
That sometimes look alike.

Life passes by so fast, Lord,
And yet how kind You are,
In granting me the precious years,
That I have had so far.
So let the days grow shorter,
The darkest shadows part,
But put the wrinkles on my face,
...And never on my heart!

Grace E. Easley

Mountain Te Deum

I thank Thee just for life,
The chance to live,
To be alive! So great Thy gift,
If Thou dost nothing give
Beside, it is enough,
To breathe Thy air,
To walk this mountain sod,
To feel the play of mighty winds,
To look Thee in the face,
And call Thee God!

From THE MESSAGE OF STEWARDSHIP by Ralph Spaulding Cushman, copyright renewal © 1973 by Elizabeth G. Stiles, used by permission.

Just For Today

Lord, for tomorrow and its needs,
    I do not pray;
Keep me, my God, from stain of sin,
    Just for today;
Let me no wrong or idle word
    Unthinking say:
Set Thou a seal upon my lips,
    Just for today.

Let me both diligently work,
    And duly pray;
Let me be kind in word and deed,
    Just for today;
Let me in season, Lord, be grave,
    In season, gay;
Let me be faithful to Thy grace,
    Just for today.

In pain and sorrow's cleansing fires,
    Brief be my stay;
Oh, bid me if to-day I die,
    Come home to-day;
So, for to-morrow and its needs,
    I do not pray;
But keep me, guide me, love me, Lord,
    Just for to-day.

Sybil F. Partridge

Life's Adventure

Life is a great adventure,
Each day a new surprise,
So sweep the cobwebs from your heart,
And open up your eyes.
Sorrow flees the sunlight,
So throw the windows wide,
And watch the brightness flooding in,
Warm everything inside.

Life is a great adventure,
For those who would explore,
The road winds upward and the wind
Taps lightly at the door.
And should the day be cloudy,
No reason to complain,
When trees along the avenue,
Are singing in the rain.

Life is a great adventure,
Each day that passes by,
A dazzling panorama
As broad as it is high.
Beyond all comprehension,
The wonder of the spheres,
When one by one the hours make
A ladder of the years.

Grace E. Easley

God Understands

God understands; it is sweet to know
When we are tired and when the hand of pain
Lies on our hearts, and when we look in vain
For human comfort, that the Heart Divine
Still understands those cares of yours and mine.

Not only understands, but day by day,
Lives with us while we tread the earthly way,
Bears with us all our weariness, and feels
The shadow of the faintest cloud that steals
Across our sunshine, even learns again
The depth and bitterness of human pain.

There is no sorrow that He will not share,
No cross, no burden for our hearts to bear
Without His help; no care of ours too small
To cast on Jesus; Let us tell Him all,
Lay at His Feet the story of our woes,
And in His sympathy find sweet repose.

Deeper

Let me try a little harder
Let me pray a little more
Let me go a little farther
Than I've ever gone before

Let me sing instead of sighing
As I pass beneath the rod
Let my life burn out for others
Less of self and more of God.

Let me see the ones about me
Hungry for the peace I know
And the spirit of my Savior
Father let me ever show

Let me lift the one who's fallen
Help the lame upon the way
Soothe the weary, calm the suffering
Knowing thou wilt come someday

Others, Lord, yes others
Let this my motto be
Help me to live for others
That I may be like Thee.

Nellie Martin

Assurance

In bitter anguish and despair
I sought my Lord,
    And He was there—
I sought Him through
    The day along;
He moved to make
    My spirit strong.
In sorrow, joy, whatever be
He lifts to bless
    The whole of me.

Roxie Lusk Smith

Dream Dreams

Dream dreams of real compassion
    And the joys your dreams could bring.
Dream dreams of their fulfillment
    And the sad you helped to sing.
Then think of ways of making
    These good dreams to come true.
The good Lord needs more dreamers
    Yes, the Lord has need of you.

He needs your hands to minister
    To the sick and insecure,
Your life to be a sermon
    How to love and to endure,
He needs your voice to tell men
    The humble Gospel story
And to spread abroad the knowledge
    Of his great love and glory.

Sister Mary Gemma Brunke

If Just One Soul

If just one soul
Has been enriched
Because you trod this earth,
Or if one doubting heart
Can trust
And realize its worth,
And turn to Christ
Because you shared
Your joy
To ease his pain,
You'll know, beyond
The slightest doubt,
You'll not have lived
   in vain!

Alice Hansche Mortenson

God's Love

God is always with me
    I have no need for words
For even in the stillness
    His love is ever heard.

His warming presence fills me
    So deep within my soul
And fills my heart with gladness
    His love does make me whole.

Dolores Karides

A Morning Prayer

Lord grant me strength to meet this day;
Please take my hand and lead the way.
Teach me trust and patience too,
In daily tasks which I must do.
When I may falter hear my prayer,
Strength is knowing You are there.

Mary H. Wittner

Only Trust Him

God knows your secret longings,
He knows your silent tears,
    and even within the shadows
His hand is on your fears.

When your head is on the pillow
    in the wee hours past midnight,
    just trust that God is with you
    somewhere within your room this night:

Watching, never sleeping,
He tends your fragile care,
    and in the quiet hours a vigil keeping
He breathes for you a prayer.

Just trust Him for the answers
    that a questioning heart can't give,
    for God holds your every tomorrow
    knowing your "each today" is His.

Roxie Lusk Smith

This Day

God forgive my angered voice
　　My wail when things go wrong,
For forgetting I am — Oh so weak
　　And only Thou art strong.

God forgive my restless heart
　　That so often strays from home,
And help me in Thee to find
　　A place to call my own.

God forgive my faltering steps
　　Amid hardships, pain and care,
Let me remember the heavy cross
　　That You were glad to bear.

God forgive my hurried steps
　　In life's preparatory way,
And cause me, God, to often stop
　　and help someone each day.

Charlotte L. Darwin

The Meaning

I will not doubt
Though there be questions in the heart;
Though eyes be damp with tears
    that course from streams within,
I will not doubt.

There is a certain strength
    that grace has given in my need,
    and hope lends inward voice
    to make my spirit strong...

I still can sing; for more and more
Christ holds the mourning heart—
There is the clasp of comfort
    that no human will can take in hand,
For, in the depths of ache
    the soul has mind to understand.

Roxie Lusk Smith

Steadfast Heart

I've dreamed many dreams
    that never came true
I've seen them vanish at dawn,
But I've realized enough of my dreams,
    Thank God,
To make me want to dream on.

I've prayed many prayers
    when no answer came,
Though I waited patient and long,
But answers have come
    to enough of my prayers
To make me keep praying on.

I've trusted many a friend that failed,
And left me to weep alone,
But I've found enough
    of my friends true blue,
To make me keep trusting on.

I've sown many seed
    that fell by the way
For the birds to feed upon,
But I've held enough golden sheaves
    in my hands
To make me keep sowing on.

I've drained the cup
    of disappointment and pain
And gone many ways without song,
But I've sipped enough nectar
    from the roses of life
To make me want to live on.

Hazel Cassens

Be True

Thou must be true thyself,
    If thou the truth wouldst teach;
Thy soul must overflow, if thou
    Another's soul wouldst reach!
It needs the overflow of heart
    To give the lips full speech.

Think truly, and thy thoughts
    Shall the world's famine feed;
Speak truly, and each word of thine
    Shall be a fruitful seed;
Live truly, and thy life shall be
    A great and noble creed.

Horatius Bonar

The Hardest Thing

The hardest thing on the road of life
Is not the length of the way,
For some it's long,
For some it's short,
The shadows at close of day.

The hardest thing and the saddest thing
That weighs upon the breast,
That brings despair,
That brings deep care,
To the one that seeks for rest,

Ah yes, dear friend, the hardest thing
Is lonesomeness we feel:
The suffering soul,
The long lost goal,
For the friends that weren't so real.

But the hardest and the saddest thing,
The lonesomeness of soul,
Is somehow gone,
Is fled from one
Who maketh Christ his goal.

He's gone before on the lonesome road;
He knows each curve and snare.
He is the way,
Eternal day;
He seeks to lead you there.

Believe in Him, reach out in faith;
Trust in His loving care.
The Christ Who died,
The Christ Who lives,
He seeks to lead you there.

Charles G. Ramsey

Life Is Worth Living

Life is worth living
    Wherever you are,
Deep down in a dungeon
    Or high on a star.

Life is worth living;
    It all has a plan
When God knows you're giving
    The best that you can.

The saint and the sinner,
    The great and the small,
We all are God's children
    And He loves us all.

So pray when you're happy
    And pray when you're blue,
For life is worth living
    When God lives with you.

                    Nick Kenny

Help Me

Help me to find someone today
    Who needs what I have to share—
A kindly word, a thoughtful deed,
    A bit of loving care.
Help me to take the time to be
    An understanding friend
To someone who needs a helping hand
On which they can depend.
Help me to love as Jesus loves—
That same unselfish way.
Help me to be like Jesus
In all that I do and say.

Vera Beall Parker

The Dreaded Task

I found the task
    that I had dreaded so
Was not so difficult
    when once begun;
It was the dread itself
    that was the foe,
And dread once conquered
    means a victory won.

Margaret E. Bruner

It Matters Not

It matters not if I've been hurt;
    It matters not at all
That sometimes from my weary eyes
    The scalding teardrops fall.
What matters most is if I've erred
    And not confessed the sin,
And through my lack some needy soul
    Has failed to follow Him.

It matters not if cherished friends
    On whom I've leaned in vain
Have wounded me by word and deed
    And left me with my pain.

What matters is — can I forgive
    Again and yet again?
'Tis not "Have they been true?" but "Lord,
    Have I been true to them?"

'Twill matter not when evening comes
    How rough the road I've trod,
If only I have walked with Him
    And led some soul to God!
For when I wake to be like Him
    Who saved me by His grace,
Earth's pain will vanish when I catch
    One glimpse of His dear face!

              Alice Hansche Mortenson

Loneliness

Loneliness may visit,
but it never can possess,
a heart where God's love lingers
and where his spirit rests.

Dianne W. Brown

Prayer For A Day's Walk

God let me find the lonely ones
   Among the throng today
And let me say the word to take
   The loneliness away:
So many walk with aching hearts
   Along the old highway.

So many walk with breaking hearts,
   And no one understands;
They find the roadway rough and ste
   Across the barren lands;
God help me lighten weary eyes,
   And strengthen nerveless hands.

God help me brighten dreary eyes,
　　And let my own grief be
A sure reminder of the grief
　　Of those who walk with me.
When words fail—hands fail—let me go
　　In silent sympathy.

Grace N. Crowell

The Artist

I love to watch
God paint the dawn
In scarlet flush and gold;

I love to watch
Him touch the sky
In colors bright and bold.

I love to watch
God paint the dusk
In purple-shadowed gray.

Then leave His name
upon it all—
Artist of night and day!

Marion Schoeberlein

The Little Road

There is a little road for all
    To follow day by day;
A road with many sign posts
    To guide us on our way.
These sign posts are for all to see,
    And they are all we need,
For the journey is a safe one
    If we go to where they lead.
This road is straight, but all along
    Are paths we may detour,
But those who are wise keep their eyes
    On the road they know is sure.
The ones who wander in the paths
    Leaving the road behind
All will learn when they would return
    The road is hard to find.
This little road is the road of life,
    And it will always pay
To follow where we know is right
    As we go along the way.

Virginia Katherine Oliver

Lead Thou the Way

Each time I speak let what I say
    Be of Thy Word,
That those who listen shall be blessed
    For having heard.

Of what I do let every move
    Be first a prayer,
That in my touch of other hearts
    I shall not err.

And when I walk my feet shall take
    Thy Chosen Way,
That those who hold my hand shall not
    Be led astray!

Esther Nilsson

Lifeline

Lord, help me on this sea of life
    Toward that Eternal City,
To not pass up the wayside ports —
    Compassion, Love, and Pity.

Oh, let me not be so absorbed
    In making a safe landing
For my small barque I'll miss the port
    Of Human Understanding.

Oh, let me not be so engrossed
    In reaching that blest goal,
I'll fail to hear the faint, far cry
    Of some lost, sinking soul.

Oh, let me not forget, dear Lord,
    That I was once lost too,
And someone took the time to point
    me lovingly to You.

Life's sea is rough, the night is dark
    For little ships that roam.
Please let me be a lifeline, Lord,
    To lead them safely home.

Alice Hansche Mortenson

Teach us, Lord, to serve thee as thou deservest:
to give and not to count the cost;
to fight and not to heed the wounds;
to toil and not to seek for rest;
to labor and not to ask for any reward
save that of knowing that we do thy will.

St. Ignatius of Loyola

The Weaver

My life is but a weaving
    Between my God and me;
I may not choose the colors,
    He knows what they should be
For He can view the pattern
    Upon the upper side,
While I can see it only
    On this, the under side.

Sometimes He weaveth sorrow,
    Which seemeth strange to me;
But I will trust His judgment,
    And work on faithfully;
'Tis He who fills the shuttle,
    He knows just what is best;
So I shall weave in earnest
    And leave with Him the rest.

At last, when life is ended,
    With Him I shall abide,
Then I may view the pattern
    Upon the upper side;
Then I shall know the reason
    Why pain with joy entwined,
Was woven in the fabric
    Of life that God designed.

Thankfulness

My God, I thank Thee who has made
    The earth so bright;
So full of splendor and of joy,
    Beauty and light;
So many glorious things are here,
    Noble and right!

I thank Thee, too, that Thou has made
    Joy to abound;
So many gentle thoughts and deeds
    Circling us round,
That in the darkest spot on earth
    Some love is found.

I thank Thee more that all our joy
    Is touched with pain;
That shadows fall on brightest hours;
    That thorns remain;
So that earth's bliss may be our guide,
    And not our chain.

I thank Thee, Lord, that Thou hast kept
    The best in store;
We have enough, yet not too much
    To long for more;
A yearning for a deeper peace,
    Not known before.

I thank Thee, Lord, that here our souls,
    Though amply blest,
Can never find, although they seek,
    A perfect rest,—
Nor ever shall, until they lean
    On Jesus' breast!

                Adelaide Anne Procter

The Loving Thing

The child in me that often wished
to wipe His brow and help Him up
    each time He fell,
now knows that wish is granted us
each time we do for any man
    the loving thing.

      Edward A. Gloeggler

Rest Thou My Mind

Rest Thou my mind in Thee, Dear Lord;
   Give to me sweet repose;
Take weary flesh and troubled mind;
   In peace my eyelids close.

I've labored in Thy fields today,
   The harvest fields to reap,
And now in quiet evening's hour,
   Give to Thy servant sleep.

I rest in Thee, complete, secure,
   For in my soul is peace,
For Thou didst wash me clean today,
   And gave my soul release.

Dear God, I thank Thee here alone,
 As on my bed I pray,
That Thou didst walk beside me
 Throughout the heat of day.

And now I rest in Thee alone,
 Nor darkest night would fear,
For in the closing of my eyes,
 I know that Thou art near.

Charles G. Ramsey

Confession

Sometimes I come to You in tears
My heart so full of pain,
Discouraged and disheartened
You pick me up again.

Sometimes I come to You in want,
I grumble and complain
And then You give just what I need
And pick me up again.

Sometimes I come to You in fear,
I fight my dread in vain
I cannot do it on my own —
You pick me up again.

Sometimes I come to You in thanks
And then it's very plain
That anytime I come to You
You'll pick me up again.

I always come to You in love,
Whether in loss or gain
You show me sweet compassion
And pick me up again.

Gretta Viney

Autograph

God wrote His autograph
Upon the sky last night
In the stars I never saw
A signature so bright!

With the dawn again
For watchers to behold—
He wrote His name in sunlight—
An autograph of gold!

Marion Schoeberlein

Human Frailty

How many times I give you my cares,
    Surrender my life and my all.
How many times do I give you my day
    And in one weak moment I fall.

How many times do I kneel and confess
    Telling you how I repent.
And before the day has come to a close
    I have the same fears and laments.

How many times have I opened my heart
    And invited my Lord to come in,
Humbly kneeling at the foot of the Cross
    And again be tempted to sin.

Helen Parker

Open My Eyes

God open my eyes so I may see
    And feel Your presence close to me...
Give me strength for my stumbling feet
    As I battle the crowd
    on life's busy street.
And widen the vision of my unseeing eyes
    So in passing faces I'll recognize
Not just a stranger, unloved and unknown,
    But a friend with a heart
    that is much like my own...

Give me perception to make me aware
    That scattered profusely
    on life's thoroughfare
Are the best gifts of God
    that we daily pass by
As we look at the world
    with an unseeing eye.

                    Helen Steiner Rice

There is One Who Knows

There is One Who knows all your heartache;
    He sees ev'ry falling tear;
His grace will bring you rich comfort
    And help all your burdens to bear.

Though your path may be strewn with sorrow,
    And lonely may be your day,
There's One Who will walk beside you
    And bring joy and gladness your way.

Though your dearest friend may forsake you,
    And loved ones misunderstand,
There's One Who will never leave you;
    He'll hold to your faltering hand.

Come, kneel at the Cross of the Saviour
    And cast your cares upon Him!
He graciously bestows pardon
    And takes away burden of sin.

There is never a disappointment,
    Nor heartache He cannot heal;
He'll answer your soul's deep longing,
    As in His blest Presence you kneel.

Kathryn Thorne Bowsher

Yesterday's Cross

The cross that pressed so heavy
    Is light and sweet today;
It lost its weight this morning
    When Jesus came my way.

The cross that looked so dreary
    A day or two ago,
Has, with His Presence, brightened,
    He helped me lift it so.

It now is light, a feather,
    I laugh amid my tears,
And raise, with Him, my burden —
    All flown my anxious fears.

The cross that weighed so heavy,
    The tears that fell so fast;
Are changed to glorious rainbow
    In skies, all blue at last!

Needless Worry

Some of your hurts you have cured,
And the sharpest you still have survived,
But what torments of grief you endured
From evils which never arrived!

Ralph Waldo Emerson

A Morning Offering

My God, I offer You today...
My life and all its care...
Keep me from sin till evening comes...
Help me my cross to bear...
My day is long, my work is hard...
My life seems all a-wry...
I have no time to think or pray...
And the years pass swiftly by...
O God, accept my work today...
I do it all for You...
'Tis badly done — complainingly...
But the best that I can do...
And You are kind and gentle, Lord, ...
And the faults You will not see...
Such as it is, my life anew...
I dedicate to Thee.

Rev. Thomas Foy

Blessing On All Our Days

May blessings be ours in the morning,
   May gladness be ours in the night,
May the breezes but gently caress us
   And the sun give us softly its light.
In stress and in doubt and in danger
   True courage and faith may we know,
And the Home Lights of God be our beacon,
   Wherever we stay or we go.

               Brian O'Higgins

We Thank Thee

We thank Thee, Lord,
That of Thy tender grace,
In our distress
Thou hast not left us
    wholly comfortless.

We thank Thee, Lord,
That of Thy wondrous might,
Into our night
Thou hast sent down
    the glory of the Light.

We thank Thee, Lord,
That all Thy wondrous ways,
Through all our days
Are wisdom, right,
    and ceaseless tenderness.

John Oxenham

Life

Life's made for living,
And giving and sharing,
Knowing and showing,
And daring and caring.
Life's made for doing,
Pursuing of dreams,
Sowing and growing,
Whatever the means.

Revealing and feeling,
And finding that you
Must learn how to take it,
To make it come true.
Along with its ups,
In spite of its downs,
Life's made of losses,
and crosses and crowns.

Grace E. Easley

God's Design

Philosophers may reason why
But I won't take the time,
I only know I'm here on earth
Because of God's design.
So I will just continue on
And do the best I can,
And know that God will do the res
Because He made the Plan.

Ed Kane

Morning Prayer

When little things would irk me, and I grow
Impatient with my dear ones, make me know
How in a moment joy can take its flight
And happiness be quenched in endless night.
Keep this thought with me all the livelong day
That I may guard the harsh words I might say
When I would fret and grumble, fiery hot,
At trifles that tomorrow are forgot —
Let me remember, Lord, how it would be
If these, my loved ones, were not here with me.

God Promised

God did not tell me,
Only roses would grow.
That I'd find no sorrow,
On the path I must go.

But He promised to be there,
Each step of the way,
Providing a way to escape,
The temptations each day.

His grace all sufficient,
Daily to see me through.
He'd help me to conquer,
And be victorious too.

Dottlee Dugan Reid

Use Me Lord

Lord, give me courage to be true
To You in all I say and do.
Give me your love to keep me sweet
To everyone I chance to meet.
Give me your power to keep me strong.
Grant me your presence all day long.
Give me the Faith that all may see
How very real you are to me.
Give me wisdom to choose the best.
Help me perform each task with zest.
Give me vision to see your plan
Use me, Lord, wherever you can.

Keep Me Near Thee

Keep me near Thee, dearest Jesus,
   Always in Thy holy sight.
Draw me ever closer to Thee
   Till the coming of the night.

Hold my hand and lead me onward
   Through the trials and stress of day:
Let me see Thee, hear Thee, feel Thee —
   In my daily toil and play.

Hand in Thine I can not falter
   Thou art ever at my side;
And my heavy heart seems lighter
   When it in Thy heart confides.

Life's Seasons

Life is like the seasons
    Each one its changes bring,
A fertile seed takes root and grows
    Thus youth is like the Spring.
Maturity comes in Summer
    As we work and play and sing,
In the Fall we gather harvest
    From the deeds we sowed, and then,
Alas too soon it's Winter
    And our eyes have grown quite dim,
Have faith no need to worry
    'Tis not the end of everything
For our souls will be returned again
    To Heaven, where God is King.

                    Louis H. Guenther

Understanding

Not more of light I ask, O God,
    But eyes to see what is:
Not sweeter songs, but ears to hear
    The present melodies:
Not more of strength, but how to use
    The power that I possess:
Not more of love, but skill to turn
    A frown to a caress:
Not more of joy, but how to feel
    Its kindly presence near
To give to others all I have
    Of courage and of cheer.
No other gifts, dear God, I ask,
    But only sense to see
How best these precious gifts to use
    Thou hast bestowed on me.

Extra Things

We thank Thee, God, for extra things
    You send along our way
Both when our days are sunny bright
    And when our skies are gray.

The little planned surprises dropped
    From Thy great, loving hand,
Like unexpected showers on
    A parched and desert land.

The meeting of an old-time friend,
    The lifting of a care,
And sunlight breaking through the clouds
    To tell us You are there.

Just why You do these extra things
    Our finite minds don't know;
It must be You delight in them
    Because You love us so!

                    Alice Hanche Mortenson

Make Life a Little Sweeter

O let me shed a little light
On someone's path I pray;
I'd like to be a messenger
Of happiness today!

It may be just a phone call,
A smile, or a prayer,
Or long neglected letter
Would lift the edge of care.

I want to spread some happiness
In what I say or do,
Make life a little sweeter
For someone else! Don't you?

Alice Hansche Mortenson

Sharing

Some share their lives with all they meet
    Along life's thoroughfare,
A smile...a nod...a silence sweet,
    These are the joys they share.

Some close their eyes along the road
    While others hold their ears,
And there are quick and thoughtless words
    That transform smiles to tears.

Our hearts tick off the nights and days
    Like clocks upon a shelf,
And lonely is the one who wastes
    God's time upon himself.

                Nick Kenny

Thou Art Near

O love Divine, that stooped to share
Our deepest pang, our bitterest tear,
On Thee we cast each earth-born care,
We smile at pain while Thou art near.
Though long the weary way we tread,
And sorrow crown each lingering year
No path we shun, no darkness dread,
Our heart still whispering "Thou art near."

Oliver Wendell Holmes

Experience

We must live through the weary winter,
　　If we would value spring.
And the woods must be cold and silent,
　　Before the robins sing.

The flowers must be buried in darkness,
　　Before they can bud and bloom.
And the sweetest and warmest sunshine,
　　Comes after the storm and gloom.

So the heart, from the hardest trial,
　　Gains the purest joy of all.
And from the lips that have tasted sadness,
　　The sweetest songs will fall.

For as peace comes after suffering,
　　And love is reward of pain,
So, after earth, comes heaven,
　　And out of our loss, the gain.

Kindness

Kindness that portrays
  A love that will endure,
Kindness that reveals
  A hope that's strong and sure.

Kindness that exchanges
  Faith enough for today,
Kindness that remembers
  A child along the way.

Kindness won my heart,
  Such kindness born of love,
Kindness that gave all
  And comes from God above.

And may I learn from Him,
  Such kindness to impart,
Strength and grace and faith,
  To another lonely heart.

Elizabeth E.S. Williams

Never Alone

Sometimes, oh Lord, when I cannot pray,
I sit very still with nothing to say.
But never-the-less, I know you are there;
I whisper your name 'cause I know you care.
You know that I'm troubled with things on my mind,
And you know I've been weak, so often unkind,
But your spirit is with me, right here in this home;
And I know that I never am walking alone.

Helen Parker

These Are The Gifts I Ask

These are the gifts I ask
Of thee, Spirit serene:
Strength for the daily task,
Courage to face the road,
Good cheer to help me bear the traveler's load,
And, for the hours of rest that come between,
An inward joy in all things heard and seen.

These are the sins I fain
Would have thee take away:
Malice and cold disdain,
Hot anger, sullen hate,
Scorn of the lowly, envy of the great,
And discontent that casts a shadow gray
On all the brightness of the common day.

Henry van Dyke

Consolation

There is never a day so dark and dreary
But God can make it bright.
There is never a night so black and void
But God can send His light.
So take to Him those hopeless things
That are tearing at your life...
The heart that puts its trust in God
Finds help to meet the strife.

Roxie Lusk Smith

Thank God For Little Things

Thank You, God, for little things
    that often come our way —
The things we take for granted
    but don't mention when we pray —
The unexpected courtesy,
    the thoughtful, kindly deed —
A hand reached out to help us
    in the time of sudden need —
Oh make us more aware, dear God,
    of little daily graces
That come to us with "sweet surprise"
    from never-dreamed-of places.

Helen Steiner Rice

Choice

Our lives are songs;
    God writes the words
And we set them
    to music at pleasure;
And the song grows glad,
    or sweet or sad,
As we choose
    to fashion the measure.

Ella Wheeler Wilcox

The Human Touch

'Tis the human touch
    in this world that counts,
  The touch of your hand and mine,
Which means far more
    to the fainting heart
  Than shelter and bread and wine;
For shelter is gone
    when the night is over
 And bread lasts only a day,
But the touch of the hand
    and the sound of the voice
  Sing on in the soul always.

Spencer Michael Free

Hymn

Lord Jesus, once you spoke to men
Upon the mountain, in the plain;
O help us listen now, as then,
And wonder at your words again.

We all have secret fears to face,
Our minds and motives to amend;
We seek your truth, we need your grace,
Our living Lord and present Friend.

The Gospel speaks, and we receive
Your light, your love, your own command.
O help us live what we believe
In daily work of heart and hand.

Prayer © 1975, ICEL, Inc.

A Guide That Never Falters

There is a Guide that never falters,
    Amidst the storms of doubt and fears —
For He has walked the way before thee,
    And He knows the path you see;
His feet have trod the rugged hillsides,
    And the valleys of despair —
His life has paved the way to heaven,
    Never fear, He'll guide you there;
His soul has tasted mortal anguish,
    His eyes have felt the sting of tears,
He's a timely guide, a sympathetic Saviour,
    So, trust to Him your future years.

Elizabeth E.S. Williams

My Task

To love some one more dearly every day,
To help a wandering child to find his way,
To ponder over a noble thought, and pray,
    And smile when evening falls.
        This is my task.

To follow truth as blind men long for light,
To do my best from dawn of day 'till night,
To keep my heart fit for His holy sight,
    And answer when He calls.
        This is my task.

                Maude Louise Ray

You Never Walk Alone

You never walk alone my friend
Though you may think you do,
For in your sorrow and despair
God always walks with you.
There is no hour, no passing day
He is not by your side,
And though unseen he still is there
To be your friend and guide.
Whene'er you think you walk alone
Reach out and you will find,
The hand of God to show the way
And bring you peace of mind.

                    Harold F. Mohn

Your Own Version

You are writing a Gospel,
    A chapter each day,
By deeds that you do,
    By words that you say.

Men read what you write,
    Whether faithless or true;
Say, what is the Gospel
    According to you?

                        Paul Gilbert